these
are
the
words

Trigger warning:

Mentions of anxiety, depression, non-graphic sexual assault and abuse, heartbreak, homophobia, biphobia, racism, misogyny, trauma and grief.

these are the words

NIKITA GILL

MACMILLAN

Published 2022 by Macmillan Children's Books
an imprint of Pan Macmillan
The Smithson, 6 Briset Street, London EC1M 5NR
EU representative: Macmillan Publishers Ireland Ltd, 1st Floor,
The Liffey Trust Centre, 117–126 Sheriff Street Upper
Dublin 1, D01 YC43
Associated companies throughout the world
www.panmacmillan.com

ISBN 978-1-5290-8360-6

57986

A CIP catalogue record for this book is available from the British Library.

Printed and bound by CPI Group (UK) Ltd, Croydon CR0 4YY

MIX
Paper | Supporting
responsible forestry
FSC® C116313

*For you and the inner child who has
always needed words of healing too*

CONTENTS

Before We Begin . . .

I cannot tell you
I have all the answers.
There are still skeletons in my closet
I haven't learned the names of yet.

Which is to say:
I'm here for you,
but I'm a work in progress
just like you.

the signs
at the
beginning of
summer

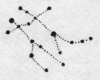 Gemini: let the sea breeze carry your heart back to you.

 Cancer: your love has always been enough, and you do not have to apologize for the ocean you carry.

 Leo: you are whole even when no one is looking at you, even when you feel like you do not exist.

 Virgo: you are not difficult for the boundaries you have set after you have survived.

 Libra: if the world feels too heavy, remember you can set it down.

 Scorpio: if the rain wants to visit your soul, then let it.

Sagittarius: you do not have to be a wildfire if you do not want to be.

 Capricorn: do not be held hostage by the fact that other people think you are too set in your ways to change.

 Aquarius: if they ridicule you for your heart, then let the moon comfort you, for you are the same as she.

 Pisces: the world is waiting for you to be ready to receive all of its beauty.

 Aries: find your sun; our fire will soon follow.

 Taurus: sometimes all you must do is feel the grass under your fingertips to know everything will be okay.

girlhood, womanhood and sisterhood

ON THE FIRST WAVE OF SUMMER

Too old for scraped knees and playgrounds
and running after ice-cream trucks.

But still young enough to sit on the docks,
feet just touching the ice-cold water,

strawberries, ice lollies and sticky fingers.
This is a litany of crushes and hopeful probabilities,

welcome to almost womanhood
and a summer of possibilities.

A LOVE STORY

You were once a love poem,
written by soft, gentle hands.
Protected with a fierceness.

Someone made you with love,
and let you out into this world.
My mother tells me the story

of a woman who gave her heart to a parrot.
One day she had to leave the cage door open.
Let the parrot fly away with her heart.

My mother told me this is what it means to love.
You put your heart in someone else.
Leave the door open,

and accept every happening
in the next minute. Whether they stay
or take your heart and walk out.

WHAT SUMMER IS FOR

Discovering your favourite film. Warm nights sitting in the garden watching the stars. Walks in the park while the sun gleams. The smell of freshly cut grass. The fragrance of jasmine. The breeze from your bedroom window. Losing yourself in the water of the ocean. Releasing what you have been holding on to since last spring. Finding new friends. Rebuilding a friendship with an old friend. Learning new things to love about yourself. Understanding that you, like the sun, were meant to burn brightly too.

CLAY

The women in your family made goddesses.
They would take the clay and mould it
between gentle fingers
until the stubbornness gave way.
The body came first, shaped by tender touch;
your grandmother always prayed
while she worked.
A wise old face, mapped by lines,
lips moving in prayer.
Maybe that's where you get it from.
The hymn placed at the nape of your neck.
The temple that lives in your eyes.
The sacred that leads your voice.
Your grandmother always said,
'From your lips to God's ears.'
She believed He was always listening,
which is why when she walked into a room
she brought a gentle peace with her.
Whoever crafted her must have
had the holiest of hands.

THE MANY MOTHERS

Soft mother. Good mother. Mother of first seasons. Mother who wishes the world was kinder. Mother who brings me autumn leaves, little crinkled yellow pieces of once sunshine. Mother who shows me winter frost and presses her fingers against it to make it melt. Mother who takes me to meet the lambs in spring. Mother who gives me the first cool shade under the tree during the hot summer sun.

Different mother. Strange mother. Mother who wishes me a version of herself. Mother who hoped for me a sunset longer than her own. Mother who hid disappointment under her pillow. Mother who held back sadness on the tip of her tongue. Mother who sent my teachers a white flag instead of believing me. Mother of surrender and tragedy.

Fine mother. Old mother. Mother of once connections. Mother I am trying to find my way back to. Mother who gave me the seasons. Mother I do not share language with any more. Mother who cries more often than she smiles. Mother who once read me bedtime stories. Mother I hurt without meaning to. Mother who hurt me without meaning to. Mother who says sorry. Mother, I am sorry. Mother, I am sorry. Mother, I am sorry.

SPACE

You've craved it for so long
that you are overwhelmed by it.

Maybe not the first day
you're away from home.

But one day, not far away,
it will strike you that you are alone.

When this hits you,
call your mum.

Tell her that you miss her.
I promise that she misses you too.

She may not be in this place, in this room.
But she still holds your heartbeat close to her own.

The soft beating still in rhythm
with yours that says,

'be/safe, be/safe, be/safe'.
In her you will always have a home.

THINGS THAT FEEL LIKE HOME

Seeing the moon on a night where you cannot see the stars.
Listening to a once-loved song you haven't heard for years. The
brief whiff of a perfume you haven't smelled since they died.
Recalling a memory your grandmother gave you. Finding the
T-shirt of a lover long gone. The smell of the rain at any given
moment. Biting into a favourite cake only your mother could
make. Finally mastering a recipe that every woman in your family
has passed down for generations. Seeing how far you have come
in your childhood bedroom. Watching the seasons change from
your window. Looking at yourself in the mirror and not seeing a
failure but a promise of tomorrow.

'YOU'RE NOT LIKE OTHER GIRLS'

It's not a compliment when you realize
how much like other girls you are.

How we all carry the same fears of alleyways
and locker rooms and rumours gone astray.

How we all know to check on our friends
and make sure they get home.

How we all see implicitly
there are places we cannot go alone.

How we all recognize the goddess in one another,
the divine knowledge that we need each other.

How we wrap our arms around each other
when no one else will because we know what hurts.

How at the end we recognize exactly
what you're trying to do when you say,

'You're not like other girls,'
when the truth is we are.

We are exactly like each other.
It's why we need this sisterhood,

because each other
is who we are fighting for.

SOMETIMES YOU MEET A WILD GIRL

And your mother doesn't like her.
There is something much too feral about her, much too
unrestrained.

But you see her as salvation.
You see her the way a deer sees another
in the forest and knows it is safe.

She will teach you everything
you did not know was possible –
the way she rattled the cage of her own girlhood

and broke free.

You long to be like her.
And for a while you too are free despite
the enormity of everything that lies ahead.

This is a different kind of sisterhood.
Where you test the boundaries of what makes
your responsibilities without fear.

She may leave. Wild things often do.
But she teaches you that you are not small but mighty.
That the truth within you is not a wound.

ON SEEING THE WOLF AGAIN

Why is it that when this story is told

I am the cautionary tale,

but you get away with being

just a wolf.

Just a villain this is expected of,

the reason why little girls don't make it

to their grandmothers' houses.

And how is it that such a wicked thing

is dismissed as That's just what happens

when you don't listen to your mother

or Maybe you shouldn't have stayed out too late

or Maybe you shouldn't have worn that skirt,

as if it is normal to meet something sinister

in the woods or on the road

or at night when all you're doing

is going for a walk to see someone you love.

The truth is we expect the survivor

to know better, but we don't demand

the same of the abuser.

And yet in the story it is not me

who fights back but a huntsman;

we only like girls who allow themselves

to be rescued.

Not ones who fight back

and rescue themselves.

And what kind of world do we live in

where we are taught to expect harm

and also take the blame for it?

What I'm saying is, the next wolf I see,

I will stand my ground.

What I'm saying is, I am done

playing by the rules of a story

I never agreed to.

IN 150 CHARACTERS OR LESS

Everything is on fire, but everyone I love is doing beautiful things
and trying to make life worth living,
and I know I don't have to believe in everything,
but I believe in that.

FOR MY LITTLE SISTER WHEN SOMEONE SHAMES HER

It does not have to be your middle name.
It does not have to be the knife
you carry in your chest.
Or the wound you press to punish yourself
for speaking out against the pain.
The worst thing that happened to you
is not just a story
you must tell yourself in the dark.
And if the currents of this cruel ocean spit you up,
you don't need to imagine yourself as only half a spark.
We were all mothered by women
devoured by this monster already
and at least once they have wished
a better future for their daughters
where we can speak fearless awake.
Where womanhood is not synonymous with shame.
Where the red river that visits is called sacred.
Where you can treat your body like it is divine,
yes, even the wreckage that has become of it.
Where you understand that survival
is nothing to be ashamed of.
Your fight is the reason you are still here.
And there is beauty in that.
Even when it is brutal.

WHEN YOUR BABY SISTER ASKS YOU IF SHE'S PRETTY

When your baby sister asks you if she's pretty, looking like the universe is weighing down her little bones with insecurity, resist the urge to say, 'Of course, darling. Of course you are.'

Tell her instead: 'Every day, I bless the stars that fell apart to allow your body's embers to glow to life.'

Tell her instead: 'In the seven billion people that exist on this planet you are the only one of your kind.'

Tell her instead: 'You are so much more than pretty. The stars that gave you to us made you to be like the sun. You are their best ever masterpiece. You aren't pretty. You are inspiring.'

HYMN FOR THE GIRLS WHO COME AFTER US

May you get home safely after nights full of wine and friends and full belly laughs.

And when you look up at the glow of the moon, when your life is more weed than flower, may you know she looks out for you.

May every song on the radio remind you that love is here – it is here and it is for you.

And may the good times be loud and long and your sorrows only fleeting.

May you always see two magpies for joy, that the birds sing for you with your heart full as you walk through gardens of sweet-smelling peonies and roses.

May successes kiss the heels of your feet as you fly to greater heights than they said you would ever reach.

May the beat, beat, beat of this world be one of safety, so you do not need to follow each other home.

May you never have to worry for your little sisters; may she not have to make a blade of herself.

May you find the kind of happiness where you do not doubt your freedom or yourself.

love

THE INVENTION OF LOVE

It begins with a look.
It should have been just a glance,
but one of you looks too long,
and the other notices it.

You'll know it is love, the way
your heart knows the moon.
You'll know it because
this is the first time

your eyes
        don't seek
                the safest exit
when you enter a room.

WHEN YOU AREN'T READY
TO SAY I LOVE YOU

There are a dozen nameless countries inside you,
whole moons you have not experienced yet.
The world is big, but within you
there is an even bigger universe,
and, no, there is nothing wrong with you
if you haven't yet begun to feel every single emotion
that makes up that big word that is love,
because here is the secret:
you can still care for someone without saying those words.
You just need to remind yourself
that it will take you time to get there,
the same way it takes years
for nature to build a river
that finally reaches the sea,
but when it is built
no one can stop it from loving the sea
for all it is worth.

LOVE IN 150 CHARACTERS OR LESS

The summer sun drips amber honey
over everything and reminds you
the world is very big and very small
and full of ways for us
to find each other and fall in love.

SOFT MYTH

You didn't ask to love a god.
Didn't ask for someone who holds the sun
in the palm of his hands,
a prophecy caught in his throat,
body used to flying a chariot through the sky.

What is this soft divinity?
The cadence of his smile,
the casual flicker of his eyebrow,
his words all-knowing,
his stories gentle retellings.

Listen, the boy may not be Apollo,
but he wears poetry on his skin,
and carries healing in his voice
and your heart tells you,
'This is all I've ever wanted,
    all I've ever been waiting for.'

TO THE GIRL AT THE BUS STOP

They say I'm not supposed to love you.
I say then why does it feel like the solar system
has parted to help you walk towards me?

I say the universe built me this life
so I could find you right here,
standing at this bus stop

with your black bag
with lime-green edges,
waiting for the same bus
at eight every morning.

I say don't tell me
love doesn't look like this:
all peach summer dresses and warm hands,
a smile like a secret caught between your teeth.

DAISIES

She wants me; she wants me not.

She is a strawberry-scented surprise,
summer flip-flops in a coffee shop.

Everything is an ever-after.
We buy a blueberry cupcake to share with each other.

She wants me; she wants me not.

We take it to the park bench
and sit among the daisies.

Through mouths blue-tinged with cupcake,
she asks me if I've ever been kissed before.

She catches me staring at her mouth,
plants her lips on mine.

She wants me, She wants me,
   She wants me.

A BLESSING FOR THOSE STILL WAITING

The 'long drives under a starry sky' kind of love.

The 'conversations at dawn and at twilight' kind of love.

The 'amber rays of the summer sun and picnic baskets' kind of love.

The 'let me hold your broken heart and show you how beautiful
   it is' kind of love.

The 'let me build you rainbows where there are wounds' kind of love.

The 'let me be your safe place and you be mine' kind of love.

The 'let's make each other stronger every day' kind of love.

That kind of love is on its way
and it's coming to you.

FROM POET TO READER

May you find someone who makes you a poet. May you find someone who shows you love doesn't have to hurt when it can heal.

ON SELF-WORTH

You are more than
what you can do for other people.
More than your productivity.
More than the joy you give others.
More than how many pieces you give away
before it feels like you have lost yourself.
You are more than the scars
and the bruises of your past,
but, most of all,
you are more
than what you tell yourself
every night,
alone in the dark,
wishing and pleading with a universe
that you do not think can hear you
to be prettier, stronger, brighter, better.
The universe already thinks of you as a star.
It knows that you are already
its wildest dream come true.
Just like this. Just as you are.

YOUR NAME

Your name is still your name
before he speaks it like it is verse,
but now you think it holds the sweet fruit
picked from a tree.

You watch him from across the room,
always looking down when he sees you,
yearning and longing, a knot in your stomach.

Suddenly, you are painfully aware
of every moment,
every second in his presence,

heart pounding,
hearing your blood rush
inside your head.

You think a boy like that
will never look at you that way,
but, darling, are you forgetting that you are the moon?

It doesn't matter if he looks or doesn't.

You still walk holding the sun between your fingertips,
a hurricane stored in a girl's body,
the stars beneath your feet.

Your name is still a spell before he spoke it.
Even after him,
all you must do
is pronounce it with magic.

LOVE IN A SMALL TOWN

It goes
like this:

She knows that I love chocolate-chip muffins
and bakes me a batch every second Sunday.

I know exactly how she likes her bubble tea
and I bring it to her every Saturday when we meet.

When we cannot kiss, we brush the sides of our hands
as we walk down the pavement, sharing a coffee.

One day, I promise her, it will be better than this.
It doesn't have to be, she whispers back. This is enough.

And I think, but it doesn't have to be.
Just imagine all the possibilities.

A WORD OF CAUTION

Nothing lasts forever.

It's not that love wasn't enough.
Love was enough and then it ends –
it has always been fruit.

Fruit is a perishable, seasonal thing.
Meant to flourish in the spring and summer,
it is either devoured,

Or left to rot.

'YOU'VE CHANGED'

Yes of course I have and so have you,

but you don't see it.

You kiss me and wonder why the leaves are dying

and I try to explain to you that

I am turning to winter,

but this answer is never good enough.

You fell in love with summer.

You fell in love with the girl who danced and laughed and sang,

and now you're wondering where she went.

You're wondering why there are snowflakes in my eyes,

why my fingers are cooler to touch.

Tell me, would you ask the autumn to stay forever?

Would you ask winter to hold on?

Do you wish for the draughts of summer to last for all time?

Then why do you expect that of spring?

THE LESSON

I once loved someone exactly how they wanted.
When they stumbled, I put my body between them and the
ground.
When they were cold, I gave them the clothes
from my own back even if I was freezing too.
Broke my bones in two to build them bridges.
Gave my own freedom up to release them from their cages.
I thought if I gave and gave that one day
they would turn round and love me back.

They smiled as they left,
taking all of my love with them,
leaving a hole in my chest so large nothing can fill it, saying,
'Silly girl.
That isn't what love is about.'

THE SHATTERING

Maybe it was the books you read as a child,
where love is a meal of desserts.

Maybe it was the way your mother
looked at your father like he was her world
and he looked at her like she was his sky.

Maybe you've watched one too many rom-coms.
So nothing prepares you for this.
How all-encompassing it is.

The way it wraps its fingers
round your still-whole heart
with such ferocity.

The first fight feels like a house of glass breaking.
You both speak shards
that are aimed to make each other bleed.

Sometimes that is it.
It is still a love story,
just one that has ended.

But if it is good and true
you walk back to each other.
Take the shards out of one another's hearts,

pick up the pieces
of your once-gleaming glass house.
And build another one out of bricks and mortar.

AFTERMATH

And one day you will bathe and watch the last of them leave your skin. You'll make breakfast and not think of the way they like their eggs. You'll eat your favourite dessert and not worry about saving someone else a piece. You'll wear the red lipstick they hate. Not bring their name up when you're out with a friend. Not call your best friend in tears over them. You'll stop wearing the T-shirt they left at your house to bed and trade it for something softer and more comfortable instead. You won't cry into the dog's fur when you see their smiling, happy pictures on social media any more. You'll close your eyes and your mind will no longer be a place you visit for memories of them. You'll sleep and your dreams will no longer be their cathedral. You'll wake up the next day and remember how brave you are. How brave you are to keep going despite the crushing weight of such love. How brave you are to stop carrying it. To finally have found a place to put it down and forget.

SOME LOVES END SOFTER

Sometimes goodbye
can taste like a festival
because you have
outgrown each other.

Even sad stories
can have happy endings;
he leaving doesn't always have
to be marred with pain.

Sometimes you hold the knife
and choose not to use it.
Sometimes you are the one
who says goodbye,
closes the door
and there is a smile on your lips
not devastation in your eyes.

Sometimes you kiss people
and it doesn't end in tragedy.

Sometimes you are not a burning building;
they are not a fire.
Instead it ends in friendship and hope.
Sometimes it ends in laughter and not tears.

And you remember someone's name
and when you speak it out loud
it sounds like:

'Thank you for letting us go.
I hope you are happy,
in love and shining
wherever you are.'

SEASONS CHANGE

You are an unrepeatable being.
and by this I mean
a symphony of stars created your bones,
you are unforgettable warmth
of the last summer's day,
the brave first gold leaf of autumn.

Remember that
as summer fades into autumn
everything is temporary.
Even when your heart is broken in summer,
eventually autumn will turn into winter
and winter will become
the second chances of spring.

the signs at the beginning of autumn

Gemini: accept that sometimes your lips are a cliff edge and the words that fall out will harm more than heal.

 Cancer: your tears aren't a mark of weakness, but a heart strong enough to express itself in an ever hardening world.

 Leo: if people do not see your majesty, your wit, your courage, that doesn't mean your virtues do not exist.

 Virgo: you do not have to radically change who you are to be accepted this year, or the next, or the next.

 Libra: may your humour and kindness guide you through every sadness that visits you; may you be present for every joy.

Scorpio: ruthlessness with yourself and those that love you is never the answer.

Sagittarius: you don't have to be the life of the party if you don't want to be. You too can befriend solitude and grow at your own pace.

 Capricorn: you're good at organizing everything, but it doesn't quite work that way with emotions, you have to feel them, great and messy, and let them go.

 Aquarius: there is always room for poems and kindnesses; they are needed now more than ever.

 Pisces: you left a star inside someone who never knew how beautiful stars are when they collapse.

Aries: you don't have to be friends with anyone who hurt you; remember your matchstick mouth was meant for burning bridges that you will never cross again.

 Taurus: you do not have to hate yourself for the stubbornness – you just have to learn how to use it as an instrument to heal yourself rather than as a weapon.

family

ON THE FIRST LEAVES OF AUTUMN

Between hot chocolate and pumpkin spice,
mellow warmth and misty mornings,

the gold of your mother shines
alongside your father's glowing smile.

Your grandmother bakes buttery cookies,
while your grandfather rakes the amber-orange garden.

In a season where everything leaves,
you learn the fine art of loving and letting go.

THIS POEM IS A LEGACY OF FOOD

This poem is my mother
carrying a bowl of cut fruit to my room
instead of apologizing.

This poem is my father
pushing a plate of samosas to me
after an argument.

This poem is my grandmother
baking a chocolate walnut cake
after my mother and she have had a fight.

This poem is my grandfather
putting freshly washed strawberries
at my father's door instead of saying sorry.

This poem is both
soft and angry,
sweet and savoury.

You will smell the spices
made of something unlanguageable
and say 'thank you'.

WHEN YOU COME OUT TO YOUR
PARENTS AND ARE NOT MET WITH LOVE

Don't think about your mother's words.
Or the fury in your father's voice.
Don't think about the sound of the siren
outside the kitchen window,
the awful silence that follows.
Don't think about the way you wish
you hadn't told them anything.
The courage it took to climb this mountain
should never be wished away;
you climbed it the best you could,
hope clinging to each fingertip.
It's not your fault the view from the top
was ugly and unyielding.
Do not consider the closet again.
It is already overflowing;
there is no more room for you to hide
yourself like a quiet secret in there.
Do not think of your coming out as ruined.
The movies will tell you that you come out only once,
but ask any queer elder and we'll tell you
you come out your whole life.
Some will be marred with spite,
but so many will be celebrated with light.
So your parents decided they can't love a queer child.

It hurts. It would, because that is a love
that should be unconditional, but it's not.
Remember that the failing is on them,
not on you.

In this moment:

know that you are not alone.
The spirits of all of us walk beside you.
Even if you feel lonely right now,
just remember there is a reason
why the pride flag is a rainbow.

WHEN YOU COME OUT TO YOUR PARENTS AND *ARE* MET WITH LOVE

If only everything
could be painted with this kind of holy,
where all that matters is how gentle love is,
how it can heal your fears
and replace them with endless courage
because you know now that
they will never stop loving you.

DARING TO DREAM UP
A DIFFERENT FUTURE

The story has already been written for you,
but you can still reject it.

If *Destiny* is the name of your book,
you are the only one meant to write it.

You are not just your mother's resilience
and your father's journey.

Human beings don't work like that.
The universe has filled you with your own purpose;

you owe it to yourself
to go and find out what it is.

YOUR MOTHER

Didn't get to follow her dreams.
Didn't get to eat the green fruit of her own abundance.

Her fate had been decided by someone else,
who said they knew what was best for her.

No one asked her,
'If you had the power to change the world,
how would you do it?'

No one told her,
'You do not have to pack away your dreams
or extinguish the fire that burns inside your eyes.'

If you need to follow your dreams for someone,
do it for her.

Do it for every foremother who once woke up
wishing she could change the world,

but was told she couldn't
because she was just a girl.

HOW TO BELIEVE IN YOURSELF IN 150 CHARACTERS OR LESS

If no one else sees you as sacred, that's when you build a temple out of yourself, your own hopes. Become your own God if that's what it takes to follow your dreams.

GOOD FATHERS

Know that while flowers can grow anywhere,
a tender heart and a giving pair of hands
make a garden the safest place for flowerbuds
to rise and meet the sun
without the fear
of being trampled
by careless feet.

ABSENT FATHER

He asks me why I don't call him as often as my mother.
I tell him she was always there when I needed her.

He tells me it's not fair
I only remember when he wasn't there,

only remember the pain and not the good times.
And don't I get it, he was out there earning.

He was working on keeping us alive.
And I ask him,

so why have children
if you don't ever get to see them?

He tells me if I dig through my memories,
he bought me my first bicycle.

I say, but it was my uncle
who showed me how to ride it.

He says, I always sent a birthday card;
I remind him that twice he forgot the date I was born on.

I ask him how come Mum had the patience for me?

HOW COME MUM WAS ALWAYS THERE THROUGH EVERY HEARTACHE?

When I fell over the first time and cried like I was the first child to
ever cry,

it was Mum who came rushing to help me,
while his voice was all I heard saying, 'Leave her be.'

He says, 'I'm here more than my father was.
You should see how I was raised.'

I tell him, 'That's the problem, Dad.
You've made this a competition

where you want to be rewarded
for doing the bare minimum.'

I remember the day I decided
to stop waiting for his love.

The day I decided I would be my own father,
that I don't have to go looking for hope

in anyone else's arms,
if I know exactly how to grow it myself.

A BROTHER NAMED WAR

A father took a boy and named him War.

Placed a millstone round his neck.

And then derided him for not being something else.

Told him the world wanted him soft,

while only showing him sharp, painful things.

Took away his flowers.

Took away his hope.

Replaced them with a gun

and an anger that has no other way to cope.

Then let him loose and let him destroy

his sisters, his mothers.

Everything that once loved him.

Everything that once made him kind.

And we looked at this boy called War

and blamed him when he became his namesake.

SHARED HISTORY

We met because our parents introduced us.
I found you kind of boring;
in the beginning you didn't do much.

I didn't know then that you'd grow up to be
both my worst enemy
and my best friend.

Because who else can I say
I share both DNA
and that glare from Mum with?

Who else can I say
I threw a whole cricket bat at one time
and he still loves me anyway?

Who else can I say
nearly gave me a heart attack
by almost dying on the football field?

Who else do I know

I can count on

and will share their space with me?

In the moment the world falls apart

I know exactly who I will call

and, best of all, who will call me.

ON BEING THE OLDER SISTER

The most common dream anyone ever has
is the one where they're falling.

The terror in their eyes
that there is nothing to break their fall,

and somewhere in your life you learned
that it is your job to break everyone's fall,

to protect them from even themselves.
You learn micro expressions as a child

to be able to determine if your parents are happy
or sad and if they're sad how to fix it.

This isn't just pressure;
this is the way of life you were taught,

to give and give until
there is nothing left any more.

You've been fixing things for everyone for so long,
you don't even notice the damage to yourself any more.

Maybe it's time to stop carrying the whole world on your shoulders.
Maybe this is time you set it down.

ON BEING THE YOUNGER SISTER

The second most common dream in the world
is flying.

What we cannot do in real life,
we dream instead.

How do I fill such big shoes?
You ask yourself every day.

How do I become my own person
when your shadow is so large it is everywhere?

You want her to stop being so good
all the time because it's killing her, but she refuses to see it.

So you do the opposite.
You take your chances, craft your liberties.

You try to take the pressure off her the best you can
and it doesn't always work because she resents you.

It will take her time to see you are trying your best to be
both your own person and her sister.

She wants to give you the moon.
If she ever did, you would happily share it with her too.

REMINDER

The way you know
your bones are dipped in courage
is when you stand up to those you love
the moment they do something
you morally disagree with.

REMINDER II

You are not too young to have morals
and principles that are different
from older members of your family.

When they say you are
'too young to understand'
it is a way for them to escape accountability.

YOUR OWN SKIN

As a child, the aunties called my sister Coal.
Coal because of the colour of her skin,
not because of her ability to become fuel,
to glow so brightly despite them.

The boys in my class called the girls dark
as an insult, as though they forgot
how the night was when the sky
was at its most beautiful.

In society the colour of your skin
dictates the way you are treated:
the lighter your skin,
the more you are respected.

It is as if our people have forgotten
that our most powerful goddess
is midnight-skinned.

When your aunties lament over your colour,
remind them that you are the sun's own child.
When the boys in class insult your skin tone,
tell them how in the sun you have always shone like gold.

When your mother wishes you lighter,
ask her why it matters,
when you share the same colours
as the goddess of destruction and time itself.

When the world makes you feel small
for the colour of your skin,
tell them Kali didn't need anyone's approval

when she burned the whole world down,
because she couldn't abide its cruelty,
and neither can you.

AN ODE TO THE AUNTIES

Call it a response to isolation,

or society failing them.

Call it the way they never got to live a youth

that should have been completely their own,

but never ended up belonging to them.

The way boundaries were used

to rein all of them in.

Call it the sting of not having control

over anything else,

other than upholding the same system

that let them down through comments like,

'Did you hear about that girl?

Dresses like a slut.

What a terrible reputation.

Such a tragedy, such a tragedy.

Who will marry her this way?

What a shame,

     what a shame,

          what a shame.'

WHEN YOU NEED BOUNDARIES

There is a storeroom inside our hearts and it is where we keep all our guilt / the guilt of knowing that even though we love our parents / we are happier when we are not in their company / A friend once told me that growing up meant that your parents go from being gods to human / that losing faith in them is a rite of passage / Once we were young enough to believe / they were both gods / that magic was real / before 'because I said so' stopped being good enough / and instead became the storm before the hurricane starts / before resentment tinged the edges of every conversation / before we knew not to question God / when once upon a time we believed in everything we were told / Now we grow older / build our own gods / and ask for respect in a way our parents aren't used to.

THE CAT ON AUTUMN DAYS

The first chill brings the cat in sooner,
and the cat always knows when you are sad.
So she tries in her cat way to make you feel better,
brings a mouse home that manages to escape,
causes chaos while your mum is trying to bake,
but also laughter where you once held sadness.

Later, she'll fall asleep on your lap,
long black tail curled round your arm protectively,
a tiny, purring, warm shape that melts away your worries.
There are people who say cats don't know how to love.
What they do not know is cats do love;
they just love differently.

THE WISH

I am at a poetry event
and a man shows me a photo of his daughter.
She can't be more than eight.
She has a crooked smile
that shows a missing front tooth
and in her hands
a triumphant painting of a red, red house
with two tall blue people and two little purple people.
It is crafted with the boundless joy
I only see children create these days.

He says,
'This is my favourite photo of her.'

He says,
'It's what I want her to be when she grows up.'

I ask him what he means.
He looks up at me and smiles.

'Happy, of course.
What else?'

the signs
at the
beginning of
winter

Gemini: you must let go of the part of you that is making each frosted day agony.

 Cancer: the world is not made to hurt you, but it will still hurt you sometimes.

 Leo: winter does not mean the sun has forgotten about how you brighten up every room you walk into.

 Virgo: it is time to release that long-time grudge that is poisoning your heart.

 Libra: you do not have to make decisions in a hurry; take your time to think them through.

 Scorpio: instead of beating yourself up on the inside, you can weep the rage out.

Sagittarius: winter does not stop whatever wants to move from moving furiously forward.

 Capricorn: the cold is a good place to reflect when you go on long walks to release your wounds.

 Aquarius: your dreaming is what is most endearing about you.

 Pisces: there is magic inside you waiting to be recognized if you just nurture it.

 Aries: just because the sun has set doesn't mean it won't rise tomorrow.

 Taurus: the fight does not have to destroy everything that you have worked so hard to build.

for
when
you
are
hurting

ON THE FIRST FROST OF WINTER

The days have become shorter,
but magical nights full of lights are longer,

and the sweet spices of the mulled wine
your neighbours are making fills the air.

You are older now by a whole year,
and you let the ice do its work of melting away pain.

You watch your breath mist against the window,
and gently write the words, 'I was here.'

FOR DAYS OF BREAKING

When you were a child,
someone you trusted taught you
that breaking was a synonym for weakness.

And because you were young enough
to believe in everything
you believed them.

You believed that tragedies
needed to be locked away
inside your spirit.

And that's what happened, didn't it?

You learned how to build galaxies
where your sadnesses became stars
that glittered inside you,

where wounds made up whole constellations.
You quickly hid them
where no one could see.

No one told you that wounds fester.
That which you leave unspoken
only serves as a cage for your golden voice.

If there was a way to unlearn suffering,
then it is this,
the fine art of breaking.

So let your tears fall free,
allow yourself the waves of sadness
that you have been keeping at bay for so long.

It is not weakness.

If you need evidence,
just look at the night sky
and know that all across the vast universe

nebulae are constantly breaking
to come back stronger
as stars that did not exist before.

YOUR FRIEND'S PAIN

I don't think any of us were built to carry this much pain,
least of all when we don't know what to do with it.

There is your pain and there is her pain
and you work hard to sift through it.

Listen, what no one tells you is
it is not your job.

It is not your job to hold other people's pain,
letting it turn into a black hole in your heart

that swallows you whole.
When your friend tells you about her trauma,

just listen, hold her close,
then leave the pain where it is

and allow yourself to let it go.

'OTHERS HAVE IT WORSE'

You aren't allowed to look at the bright morning sky because
for someone else the sky is a dark, cold night. You cannot smile
because someone out there may be crying. You aren't allowed
to be astonished by life because there are people who refuse
to be astonished by it. You aren't allowed to breathe because
somewhere else someone has stopped. You aren't allowed to fall
in love because someone's heart is breaking.

Stop.

It's okay to experience joy even if the world feels like it's falling
apart.
It's okay to experience joy even if the world is ending.
It's okay to allow yourself happiness even when life is hard.

FOR THE DAYS YOU FEEL UNHEARD

In a world designed in such a way
that the loudest voice in the room
is treated as the most valuable

I hope you remember the quiet of the trees.
How they stand there,
tall and listening,

home to everything that sings
and grows, a beacon of loss in winter
and lush hope in the summer.

When the wind blows through them,
they serenade us with this gentle
    folk song,
their most ancient secret:

You do not have to be loud to be heard.
You do not have to be loud to be brave.
You do not have to be loud to be beautiful.

Nothing is expected of you,
other than growing
in the most sacred of ways.

FOR WHEN YOU ARE TIRED OF BEING CALLED STRONG

After it happens, your friends will call you strong.
And strangers may call you strong.
Everyone who hears will use words like that,
'strong', 'strength', 'resilient', 'brave',
and you will tire of them.

You will want to peel off your skin and discard it,
ask someone to trade bodies with you
so you can remember what it feels like to be normal
instead of this hero everyone is determined to make
of the worst thing that has ever happened to you.

It's hard to explain how your body feels like
a broken bowl that everyone keeps fixing with glue
and then turning away the side that shows the damage,
looking at the pretty side admiringly and saying,
'Look, it's as good as new.'

But it doesn't work like that.
Trauma knows where you live.
It knocks on your door when you least expect it,
finds you at a friend's birthday or wedding,
in the bathroom when you are getting ready,

in the arms of a lover in the middle of a movie.
To the people who are living with the aftermath,
know that it is okay not to be strong for anyone.

That you are still a survivor,
when your body's wracked with sobs,
Hiding under your blanket,
wishing you could disappear.
That doesn't make you small.

WHEN THEY SAY YOU
SHOULDN'T TALK ABOUT IT

Remember that the only bridges
not worth burning are the bridges
you feel safe enough to cross
because the people on the other side
have seen you after the wildfire,
after the ashes of who you were,
watching the embers of who you are becoming,
and continue to love you through it all.

SALT AND SUGAR

The thing is, I still believe in it. The sky during its thunder. The
sea during her storm. The earth during its darkest hours. You.
Yes you, reading this. I am tired of us abandoning the parts of
ourselves we do not like and calling ourselves lost things. The
sun does not abandon us when a storm visits. The sea does not
abandon the cliffs because they are hardened to her touch.
I am asking you not to abandon the parts of yourself that are
in need of more love. I am asking you to hold the parts of you
that shatter, that scare you, close. I am asking you to become
better at loving those portions of yourself you wish to abandon –
to learn from them as much as you learn from everything about
you that you love. The salt and the sugar. The gentle ocean
and the coarse sand.

WINTER

Doesn't have to be only darkness.
It is also about snowmen and winter dances.

It is about leaving the past buried in the snow
or freezing a good memory into a snow globe,

something you can turn to when you are sad,
something to hold on to in the darkness

that keeps you warm like the sun
even in the worst winter storm.

SURVIVAL

1.

You have learned to dislike yourself after it happens and there is no explanation for it when you are not the one who has done the hurting; you are the one who has been hurt. It seems unfair, because it is. You have to pick up the pieces of your broken heart, put them back together, hold yourself on the nights that you cry or through the nightmares that they leave behind. It is you who flinches when a door slams, who shudders when you hear certain words; there are haunted houses out there that you know are sturdier than you. Being unkind to yourself about the trauma is easy, because you are the only one here still listening. But give yourself some credit. Even when your scaffolding is crumbling and the ghosts of what they did to you haunt you from within, you awaken every morning and fight through another day. I know you think that isn't what courage looks like. But it is. Oh, but it is.

2.

You would rather choke on your own tears, feel your teeth rattle in your throat, drink a whole bottle of mayonnaise, spend a night listening to wailing cats, spend ten days straight fighting with your brother, relive the pain of that broken arm than think of them again and still now when the moon is full and its light so soft and the night breeze gentle, thoughts of them visit you in the dark.

3.
You feel like a match that has already been struck, used for its light and fire and then discarded.

4.
You wish them the same pain they gave you. You wish them hurricanes and thunderstorms. You wish them a drowning in their own soul. You will them anything but peace, and even through this you feel like it was all your own fault and curse your soft heart for loving this hard. If love hurts this much, you promise yourself, you don't want it ever again.

5.
And one day you will realize that, no, maybe what they did to you won't leave. But the cliffs are still beautiful even after all they have weathered at the hands of the wind and the ocean, and so are you. So are you.

THE OCEAN IN YOU

Every time you think you are broke,
know this:

no one can break an ocean.
All you are doing is breaking through

the glass that is holding you imprisoned,
diving deeper into your very own depths,

discovering yourself in the pockets
of the most sombre waves,

rebuilding your heart with coral,
with seaweed, with moon-coloured sand.

So stop trying to hold yourself back
inside the glass; it was never meant to hold you.

Instead, break it, shatter into a thousand pieces,
and become who you are meant to be,

an ocean, proud and whole.

WHEN YOU HATE YOURSELF FOR REVISITING OLD WOUNDS

You revisit old wounds for the same reason
birds will come back to the places
their nests have been destroyed.
The mind walks into the same room
because it wants to know how to fix
those floorboards, paint the walls,
turn this into a more habitable place
if it tries something different from the last time.
This is survival.
This is learning how to live through pain
once the skeletons have decided to walk out
of the closet and refuse to go back in again.
Call it the worst story you have ever owned,
a car crash within your bones
that you cannot stop staring at.
But the only way to understand pain
is to look at it and feel it
without turning away.
There is no shame in this.
Eventually, it can scab over and heal.

THE CRACKS

There are cracks inside you
that you have never even known.

That's how the grief gets in and leaves.
How the tragedy comes to visit, then slips out.

How the happiness makes its grand entrance
and sudden escape.

You can search all four corners of your soul,
but they'll find a way to hide just beyond your reach.

So perhaps you can name them.
These gentle animals who take over your heart.

This too is a part of living.
Learning how to look at your own soul,

baptizing every sparrow and raven
that comes to stay

without closing the windows
they use to fly in from

just so when you have felt everything
they have to give

they can fly back out again.

THE HAPPENING

I was wrong, by the way, about porcelain.
There is an entire art form dedicated
to fixing broken objects with lacquered gold,
so that they are even more exquisite than before.

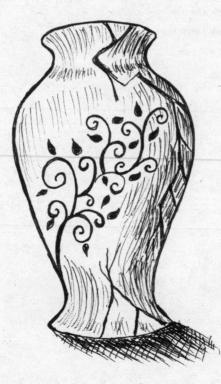

FOR WHEN YOU NEED
VALIDATION FOR YOUR ANGER

You are angry and anxious
because you never agreed
to live in a burning home
while the people who should care
pretend the fire doesn't exist.

Distress is a valid emotional response
to injustice.

for
when
you
need
to
protest

SHOUT-OUT

To lady sharks that eat their mates
if their mates pester them a little too much.

To female Komodo dragons
who are capable of virgin births.

To grandmother elephants and orcas,
the old battleaxes who always lead the herd.

To male seahorses who carry the eggs
to term and give birth to them.

To lionesses for always being the ones
who bring home the bacon
– without exception –
all while nurturing the young of other lionesses too.

To the queen bee that keeps every hive alive and to every
female bee that does all the work to generate honey.

To all the girls who have woken up
thinking their lives are over
because they have been taught
to give and give and give until nothing is left of them.

To all the girls who have broken the expectations,
the norms, what was expected of them.
To all the girls who have dreams of being somebody,
we won't let those dreams go to waste.

To all the girls who came before us,
we will evolve and revolt
and make this world a better place.

REMINDER III

The future still belongs to you. Even if they try to tell you that you are too young to understand, remember all living things need air to breathe and food to eat and a planet still full with both. You deserve a world that keeps you safe, no matter who you are, where you come from. You deserve a future filled with hope.

ON GOOGLING MICROAGGRESSIONS

What does it mean when someone asks you

where you are really from?

What does it mean when your teacher

calls you 'articulate for your kind'?

Why do people say I 'speak English so well'

when this is where I grew up?

Why do people always want to touch my hair?

What do people mean when they say

'you're not like the others'?

Why did my PE teacher say

that I 'hit well for a girl'?

Why do the boys in my class

always get away with picking on me?

Why do people always stare at my headscarf?

What do people mean when they say

they 'don't see colour' when they look at me?

Why did my head teacher call me

'a credit to my race'?

Why won't my parents talk to me about this?

Is it racism or is this all just in my head?

Am I allowed to speak about racism?

Or should I keep quiet instead?

WHAT GOOGLE DOESN'T TELL YOU

Racism is ugly and takes many forms:

people asking you where you are from,

or saying they don't see colour,

or making differences between girls and boys

from when you are very young.

And the truth is

you may feel powerless,

but if it feels wrong, then it feels wrong.

Don't let anyone make you feel

you must make yourself small

to make someone else comfortable.

That is not what your ancestors fought for.

YOUR FIRST PROTEST

It'll be the first time that you realize
you and your parents come from difference

when they tell you no, you cannot go.
But this is a cause you believe in so strongly.

You can feel rebellion coursing through your veins.
This is where you disobey.

This is where you go out and find yourself
swept up in a tide of people who believe in what you do.

Isn't it wonderful to know
that you do not stand alone.

That there is an ocean of people
marching by your side,

holding you up
even when the people you love

do not stand with you.

THE WORD IS GIRL

Six years ago,
I read a tweet that asked,

'How old were you when you were catcalled?'
Some women said twelve and some said thirteen,

and then someone said seven.
I suppose this is the part where I should say I was surprised,

but I wasn't, because for me,
it was five.

And then I stopped and considered
how this too had become its own rite of passage.

The age where you learn for the first time
how the skin you are in is public property,

the age where you learn everything is a tightrope
and you are an acrobat always on the precipice of a fall.

This is the age where you learn
telling your parents about the catcall

means a lessening of your freedom.
They'll say they trust you but not the world,

and yet it's not the world that must give up
walking the fastest way to school
because the grown man living on that street
won't stop being inappropriate with you.

You are taught the best thing to do is run
when you are barked at,

when everyone knows a predator loves the chase
and a girl who outruns her hunter is rarely praised.

We learn early what the word 'girl' means,
and it is to make the macabre look pretty.

At thirteen we know to shout fire instead of rape
when we are attacked because burning buildings

are worth more than our bodies.
At fourteen, we have been sent back home

because our shoulders are cathedrals of distraction
for our male classmates and their education.

At fifteen, we have stitched whole whisper networks
about which boys and male teachers and coaches

and friends' fathers and uncles to avoid.
At sixteen, we have heard so many stories about rape

that we no longer think 'if it happens to me',
but live in fear of 'when it happens to me'.

At seventeen, we are used to social-media conversations
about women's rights being interrupted
with 'not all men', 'what about false rape allegations'
and 'slut' and 'bitch' and rape threats abundant.

At eighteen, we know what using our voices can cost us,
so we begin every question with sorry.

We have been taught to use our politeness as a shield
when it is also the gun we could die by.

We make sure we add just enough exclamations and emojis
because we know what can happen if someone misconstrues our
words.

We have been taught to use
our politeness as a shield

when it also unsheathes swords;
that one time you smiled too much,

and that guy took it as an invitation,
and followed you for days.

And the memory of the last boy you rejected
spread rumours about you sleeping around.

And the recollection of the man who heard the word no,
but thought that was just how good girls said yes.

This isn't survival, this is defence mechanism,
a body that is always ready for a war,

which will happen when we least expect it.
The trigger is on the word.

The word is girl.
The word is RUN.

VOTE

Because nothing will change
unless you fight for it,
believe in it,
campaign for it,
hold it with the same love
with which you hold your own ambitions,
your own dreams.

WHEN THE ELECTION RESULTS ROLL IN AND THEY AREN'T WHAT YOU HOPED FOR

1. The disappointment in your belly is not the answer, even if it feels like the walls are closing in, that your grief is endless.

2. Your fear has purpose. It means you tried to circumvent future harm, but you did not succeed – but it also means that fear is the inner fuel you need to effect change.

3. The anger you feel is justified. Especially when you see people gloat over the results that you know will bring harm to your gender, religion, race or sexuality.

4. Do not allow the anger to consume you. Instead, grieve today. Scream. Punch a pillow. Cry. Do what you need to, for tomorrow you must rise and fight again.

5. Call your friends. I promise they are as sad as you are over this. Remember that sadness and defeat are not the same.

6. Do not let the rage and disappointment and sadness curdle into inaction. Instead, let them rise inside your belly as hope, and fight.

7. The world belongs to you more than it belongs to any adult. You are a forest at the very beginning of your life. They are winter while you are spring.

WHAT WE HAVE NAMED IMPOSSIBLE

Yes the ice caps are melting,
and temperatures are rising,

floods and storms are becoming a norm;
things are bad – I won't lie to you –

but still every morning
the doe and her fawn arrive through the mist

and the magpies dance carefree across the sky.
The willow near the lake sways gently,

and when I go to the seaside,
the seagulls squawk and bully us all

for food equally,
as if to say,

'It is only impossible
if you don't fight to be alive.

The sea never stops wearing the rocks down,
and they may be smoother now, but they survive.'

ON THE FUTURE

It is not easy to inherit a fractured planet
when all you have seen are the ruins.
Where do you start to rebuild
when it is others who have destroyed?

When you look to the future,
think of the forest after a wildfire.
It seems that all is ash and destruction.
It may not look it, but after a wildfire

is when the soil is most fertile.
New seeds take root and grow into saplings
that become trees and one day
that same forest will have a verdant canopy.

What I'm trying to say is,
though it may not seem it right now,
history says that after great periods of adversity
come great periods of prosperity.

The younger you are,
the more joy you will see.
You will grow your own forests
and find your peace in its trees.

FOR WHEN YOU HATE YOUR ANGER

Anger is wedged inside my bones. I keep being told there is no place for it in this world, that only good can live here, yet all around me I see harm. I see hurt. I see the existence of all things that I was brought up to believe should not exist because we are supposed to be here to help each other. Some days I cry on the phone to my mother. Some days I ask her if goodness is simply a fairy tale. Am I too late to change the world? Am I allowed to still? Am I allowed to hold this fury strong in my chest, roaring like a lion in a cage wanting to escape? My mother says to me: 'Good, you're angry. Stay angry. Now tell me how you plan to use it to make this world a better place.'

A MANIFESTO TO PROTECT MY PLUS-SIZE FRIENDS

1. When you feel uncomfortable in your chair, I promise I will stand with you.
2. When people make fatphobic remarks, I will go to war for you to remind you that you are a queen with your own army.
3. When strangers online harass you and try to tell you it's about being healthy, I will step in and tell them they are not your doctors and to back off.
4. When you feel like you cannot eat, even when you are hungry, I will hold your hand and remind you that food is good for you.
5. When even your own family lets you down by being cruel, I will be your family and remind you how loved you are.
6. When we go out in a group, I promise I won't neglect you for a crush, and when someone likes you back I promise to cheer you on.
7. When you struggle with your self-confidence, call me and we will go walking on the beach, and look at the vastness and beauty of the sky and the ocean and the sun so that we both know these are the things that make us.
8. When another celebrity goes viral for losing weight, and her body becomes a national debate, call me, friend, and I will be your safe space, your reminder that you are loved. You are beautiful. You are beautiful. You are beautiful.

ANOTHER STORY

You didn't like the last story in your life's book,
so you wrote yourself another one.

In this story,
you do not wear your body as an apology.

Instead you wear it like a quiet revolution;
you carry the future in the back pocket of your jeans.

Say girl, say glory;
each step forward is an amen.

for
when
you
hate
your
body

POEMS FROM ALTERNATE UNIVERSES

1.
In this one, we all listen to our bodies.
We eat when we want to,
we sleep when they tell us to,
we prioritise rest.

The sky is under our feet,
and the ground is above us.
We take walks on the clouds together
and the rain flies upwards into our hands.

2.
In this one, everyone has a good mother,
the kind that loves you for who you are,
holds your hand through all the hard times,
never places conditions on her love.

The sky is almost always blue;
we see the moon and the sun together often.
The world feels like a summer day
caught in the most perfect June.

3.
In this one, everyone has a good father,
one who doesn't leave when things are tough,
or disown you when you come out,
or force you to become who he wants you to be.

The sky is green and turquoise here.
The stars dance across the emerald and sapphire,
everything is a celebration when you come out.
God sends a rainbow just for you.

4.
In this one, no one hates themselves.
People look at the mirror
and see only blessing after blessing.
There is no sickness, no plastic, the air is clean.

The sky is so blue it looks like it knows no clouds.
Even the ocean, pristine purple and blue and green,
says, 'You are loved, you are loved,
you are loved.'

5.
In this one, we have no bodies.
We exist only as spirits, no genders or sexes,
finding each other across the air.
Heartbreak doesn't exist, only peaceful letting go.

We are the sky here,
free of our bones and free to fly.
No one needs a home to survive.

We are the folk songs trees whisper,
each one a chorus of,
'You need only love,
you need only love to live
and here you are alive.'

AN ODE TO BODY HAIR

My body, then young and gentle,
knew it is fertile ground for forests.
Forests of dark hair grow to protect me,
and still I am told to get rid of this canopy.
That I am not beautiful unless smooth.
At school I am made fun of for my moustache,
and so I learn the first test of womanhood,
the cutting down of these trees as sacrifice
to a goddess invented by the patriarchy.
She with her smooth skin and long hair,
perfect features and hourglass body,
curves in all the right places,
the woman they demand me to be.

No. I will no longer bleach and wax
and laser my body to fit into their moulds,
I am not going to hollow myself out
for the uses of someone else.
This body is a gift to reside in,
every feature an idea from your soul,
because that's what it found beautiful.
I will build my own goddess,
one that looks like me, limbs of forest hair
and eyes full of stories.

A SONG FOR DARK SKIN

Fall in love with this skin.

Call it midnight.

Call it the last song of a mynah bird's throat.

Call it a blackbird's wing.

Call it glittering onyx.

Call it peaceful abyss.

Call it burning and amber.

Call it fire and gold.

Call it the earth you came from.

Call it the blessing the sun gave you.

Call it the gift from the ocean's depths.

Call it the universe, which thrives in the dark.

It is already holy.

Don't let them convince you

that you are anything other than sacred.

INSTAGRAM

I scroll through Instagram and see the words 'you are beautiful as you are' right after which a perfect picture of a perfect girl in a perfect black bikini bewitches me. I wonder, 'When was the last time you had your heart broken?' I wonder, 'Has someone ever taken you stargazing and been surprised by how much you know about the constellations?' I wonder, 'Have you ever dug through the graveyards of your past thinking if you left something living in there, something you wished you had left to grow?' Her caption says 'I love the sun #beachparadise #beachbody' and I wonder if she has ever sat in the rain, letting her tears mingle in the water, whether her version of paradise was always perfection, colourized just so, a filter making it brighter, a story told flawlessly. My fingers hover over the comment button. There is so much I want to know. But instead I log out and put my phone away for the rest of the day.

MANTRAS FOR SELF-LOVE

1.
The world was made to hold you.
No matter what weight you are,
it still loves you.

That should count for something.

2.
Your body is meant to change.
It is meant to grow and take up space.
And you are supposed to evolve
your love to fit yourself
at every size you are.

3.
Other people's ideas of beauty
do not have to be wounds
you hold inside your heart.

4.
Your weight is not a condition
on how much love you deserve.

You are worth planets full of love
and kindness and warmth
and desire.

MAYBE I DON'T BELIEVE IN HEAVEN, BUT IF I DID . . .

In heaven it's always Saturday morning, with blueberry pancakes and fresh coffee with cream. And it's always Friday night sitting across from a lover and enjoying delicious home-made linguine and glasses of sweet white wine from the halls of Olympus itself. It's always Sunday afternoon with your family, eating your mum's delicious butter chicken and creamy dal makhani. In heaven it is always Friday night. Not Saturday, midnight drinking and joy rides, or Sunday, lazy breakfast and blankets – but Friday night. In heaven there is forgiveness for every lie you told yourself to keep surviving. In heaven there is rebirth for the song that you once forgot within your soul. And in heaven you are worthy, even if the person told you that you are too much. In heaven there is music. And you are your own god. Of all things small and big and forgotten and unremembered.

Which is to say, everything about my heaven is built around food and forgiveness.

Which is to say, paradise is the name of everything you wish you had given yourself in the land of the living when you felt at your most hopeless.

WHAT THE BODY REMEMBERS

This body remembers hate better than love

and whose fault is that but my own for thinking

that hate is a worthier memory than the moments

when it has protected me from sickness,

helped me win a race and climb a mountain,

given me a peaceful night's sleep,

made me rest when I needed it,

kept me awake for that all-nighter,

lifted me up more times

than it has let me down

and still I torture it

by keeping food out of its reach,

or by throwing up when I eat,

or by making it work through pain,

by ignoring its cries of hunger.

I wonder if my body would ever forgive me

for the harm I have brought to it

even when it has done nothing

but forgiven me.

PRETTY IS A LIE

What if I told you, the word 'pretty' is a skin-deep,
six-letter prison they put you in.

They say, 'If you lost weight, you'd be so pretty.'
They say, 'If your skin was clearer, you'd be so pretty.'

But what they really mean is, 'If only you looked
like our mass-produced ideal, you'd be so pretty.'

Let me tell you a secret they do not want you to know:
nothing about you is pretty and nor will it ever be so.

You see, pretty is too small and simple a word to capture
the exquisitely complex human phenomenon you are.

Every atom of you was plucked in the quiet
cosmic moments between supernovas and stars,

a carefully chosen palette of your skin, your eyes,
your muscles and bones from sunsets and skies.

So when they tell you about how pretty you could be if only—
Cut them off and say 'pretty' is not your worth or value
nor what you have ever aspired to be.

WHAT I WEIGH

I weigh the sea,
I weigh the storm,
I weigh a thousand stories long.
I weigh my mother's fortitude and my father's eyes,
I weigh the way they look at me with pride,
I weigh strength and fearless and the warrior in me.
I weigh all the pain and trauma that made me see
that I have more galaxies inside me than tragedies.
We all weigh joys and darkness and goodness and sin;
you see, we are infinite within this skin we are in.
So when you are asked what you weigh
you don't need to look down at any scale.
Instead simply tell the truth:
tell everyone how you
weigh whole universes
and storms and scars and stories too.

OUR BODIES AS ART GALLERIES

I want to take our museum bodies and turn them
into art galleries to show us how lovely we are.
I want to dust off the fingerprints of old lovers,
take down the signs that name our bodies ancient history,
turn every wounded object inside us into something
that can still be looked at and seen as beautiful,
not an object from an era we are glad
we are not living through any more.

I want us to love ourselves like we love art.

I want whole gallery walls dedicated to our soft hearts,
vermilion and crimson and indigo
across canvas after canvas framed in gold.
I want sculptures
made from the tears
we cried over losing everything.
I want our skins to be a celebration:

The texture is what makes this art,
all these lines and blemishes
and spots that show the artist's love.

I don't want us to look at ourselves
as forgotten things we hate any more.
I want us to look at ourselves and see art.

AN AFFIRMATION

My body is perfect as she is,
a glowing orb in the universe,
crafted from the hearts of falling stars,
forests upon forests growing across my skin,
rivers full of love-water flowing
through my veins.

When I need to fight, she gives me iron,
enough to be a warrior.
When I need strength, she nourishes me,
reminds me that I can do anything.
When I need joy,
she fills my head with pleasant memories.
She gives me everything I need
exactly when I need it.

My body is more than
the blood of a dying star.
She is the reason I am a whole galaxy,
dancing across the darkness
both in this moment,
and forever.

the signs
at the
beginning of
spring

Gemini: nature has never stilled itself for anyone, and neither should you.

 Cancer: this is your season to blossom into everything you have always feared.

 Leo: even lions love the flowers; there is no weakness in admitting your tenderness.

 Virgo: the sun that beams in through your window is telling you now is the time to become who you need to be.

Libra: you do not have to overthink the way you are perceived; you are loved even in indecision.

 Scorpio: you survived the most painful of winters and you deserve the kindest of all springs.

Sagittarius: this is the season for rebuilding what you thought you destroyed, for there is still hope there.

 Capricorn: some chaos is actually good for the soul if you let it in a while.

 Aquarius: all your rituals of healing and letting go have not gone unnoticed and here is when they come home.

 Pisces: you are the seed that grew despite all the odds into the resilient rose you are now.

 Aries: not every war needs to be fought with guns; some can be won through flowers.

 Taurus: you are allowed to get it wrong sometimes; mistakes are how people grow.

for
when
you
need
to
heal

ON THE FIRST FLOWERS OF SPRING

The thrush is building a nest
right outside your bedroom window,

and the freshly thawed breeze
brings hope into your now green garden.

The flowers you planted last year
sing in yellow and pink blooms.

Spring and you are soulmates,
life blossoming everywhere for you,

filled with healing and promise.

REMINDER FOR HEALING

You do not owe anyone your forgiveness.
The trees do not apologize to the wind that uproots them.
The rocks do not apologize to the erosion by the sea.
The stars do not apologize to the universe
when they are writhing and dying out slowly.
And you are not obligated to forgive anyone
but yourself.

THE WAY OUT

Do not allow him to consume you. If he does not call, go to sleep. If he does not message, put your phone away and have a fantastic day anyway. If he acts distant when you are with him and refuses to tell you what is wrong, don't wait for him. Go home and do something you love. If he tries to insinuate you do not need your friends now that you have him, spend more time with your friends. If he tries to teach you a lesson through the silent treatment, ignore him completely.

If he plays with your feelings constantly, walk away from him. If he acts like your body is his entitlement when you are not ready, walk away from him. If he says terrible, unforgivable things and threatens to leave you after every argument, walk away from him. If he forbids you from doing anything you love, walk away from him. If he claims ownership of your accomplishments, walk away from him. If he demeans you or disrespects your being a girl and refuses to stop when you tell him it hurts, walk away from him.

I cannot stress this enough: you live for yourself first. He is a secondary character in the story of your life. Do not allow him to turn you into a secondary character in your own book.

HEALING IS NOT LINEAR

It knows how to take its time.
So be patient with yourself,
for you, like the earth,
need the same nourishment
and time that it takes flowers
to bloom, wilt,
and bloom all over again.

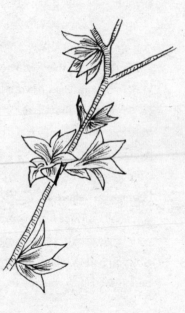

IN TIMES OF TRANSFORMATION

Treat the loneliness like it is a prophecy. Allow the hunger to come. Then nourish your body with everything you have been denying yourself. Stretch. If you grow, your skin is ready for it. Allow the moon in through your window. Sit with it awhile and lament about how hard this is, but do it anyway. The moon will call you brave. It's the highest compliment it has ever given anyone. Accept it graciously.

You are not doing this wrong. No one teaches the fish how to live underwater; they just know how to. That's what growth is to human beings. Discard your last skin. Gently pack away the old versions of you that do not serve you any more. When you allow transformation, it may feel like a cruel goddess, but it's simply being firm.

People you believe are necessary in this time will leave. When you finally surface from your chrysalis, hard-won beauty between your fingertips, butterfly wings at your back, you will understand why you had to release anything that did not serve you. Some people walk into your life to be let go.

EVERY DAY

Is not an opportunity to improve yourself.
Some days are just there for you to accept yourself
and look at the clouds.
This too is growth.
This too is rising.
Just existing is enough on some days.
The flowers do it every day
and make the world more beautiful
just by being here.

So do you.

Rest today.
There is tomorrow.

FOR WHEN THEY CANNOT LOVE YOU FOR WHO YOU ARE

Be careful of the people who demand
you must stop burning brightly for them to stay.

That they can only love you
once the flames have become embers.

That your wildfire ambition is too much of a burden.
Remember that the ashes make your bones fertile

for what you want to grow.
You are not the problem here.

Fire is still glorious,
orange flames dancing.

When I was a child,
I was drawn to the burning of all things.

Like a moth, I was drawn to endings
more than beginnings.

It took someone loving the flames in me to understand
that even hardened and ash, I am still worthy of love.

You too are still worthy.
Especially while you burn like a comet through the sky.

HOW TO HEAL FROM THE PAIN

Someone may tell you your hurt is a small thing,
and, yes, we are all small,
just a flutter of a butterfly's wings
in the grand scheme of the universe,
but we are also the heartbeat of this planet,
the sound of the birds at dawn,
the colours of the sky
that is never the same shade twice.
Listen: if you put your ear to a tree's trunk,
maybe you can hear it grow.
And all of this is to say,
it is worth something to be here,
to be alive and have all these small gifts,
moments that you catch in your palms
where you look in wonder and are astonished
by the abundance you see.

LESSONS FROM THE WILD

On my walks in the woods I see the robin fly brazenly,
unafraid of who is looking.
I watch the blackbird make its nest on the lowest branches,
fearless of what humans may think of it.
I crouch to watch the dappled fawn from between long grass,
skipping with delight across the woods she considers her own.

I envy the wild.
Do you think the stag ever stops to doubt its own majesty?
No. Like the river from which he drinks,
he just knows.

**for
friendship
and
found
family**

THE TEST

Somewhere along the way we decide
to test the waters of our friendships
with a secret.

You trust them with the worst thing
that happened to you and
see if they can keep it.

A dangerous game
where you try to picture
how this story ends,

your heart beating so fast
your body feels spent.
Trust feels like praying.

Hope feels like knowing
your secrets are safe
between the synapses of someone

who once watched the stars with you,
held your hand,
but asked for nothing more.

This is the oldest love there is.
No one teaches us how to do it.
It is simply remembering

and knowing how not to betray each other.

REMINDER ON FRIENDSHIP

Some friends are temporary,
not because you hurt them
or they hurt you.

But because friendships
are like seasons sometimes.

Outgrowing a friend may hurt,
but it's something you must do.

Every meadow
must let go of its flowers in winter,
so it can grow fresh ones in spring.

SANCTUARY

We may not know much,
but we know to save each other a seat everywhere.

That seat isn't just a seat;
it's an ode to someone we know gets it.

And when the world
turns its back on us

we have each other's back,
because that's what friendship is.

It's the time
that someone tried to push you to the ground,
but your friend pushed them back.

It's the time
your mother threw you out of the house,
but their family welcomed you in like you were their own.

It's the first time you fell in love
and they were there to hear you talk
endlessly about their hair, nose, eyes and ears.

It's becoming someone's favourite sanctuary
when they have both a hundred places they could be,
and when they have nowhere else to go.

ON THOSE CONVERSATIONS YOU CAN'T HAVE WITH ANYONE ELSE

My friend asks me if I know how to hide my feelings yet. I ask her what she means and she says, 'You know that to live is to know how to hide parts of yourself, right? That you must show certain faces to certain people, and that's how you survive.'

I think of how the river holds her hands out in prayer to the ocean. I think of how the cliffs cry out to the ocean unflinchingly to return and how she only comes when she wants to, not when she's called. I think of the ocean's depths, how she faces countless sea storms, then take my friend's hand, squeeze it and say, 'No, actually. I've never thought of survival that way at all.'

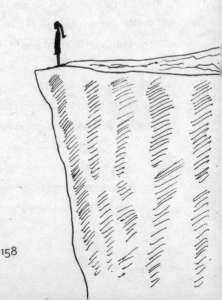

HANGING OUT

I don't think I've ever been happier
than when I'm hanging out with you
and you tell me the silliest story about your day.

Tell it again
so we can become cascades of laughter
for the third time today.

GIRLCODE

'I don't know what I would do without you'
means I don't know if I'd still be here without your love.

'He didn't deserve you'
means you deserve a gentle god and he wasn't sacred.

'Come over and we'll do homework'
means we'll sit and talk about everything but.

'Let's go shopping'
means I'd rather spend my day with you and no one else.

'Be careful'
means if he breaks your heart I will grind his bones to dust.

'Sit next to me'
means we can protect each other.

'You're my best friend'
means you're the sister I chose.

'Call me when you get home'
means I love you.

'Tell me you're safe'
means I love you.

'It's okay to cry – I'm here'
means I love you I love you I love you.

ON THE REAL ONES

Maybe the real lesson is the friends we made along the way. No, but for real, maybe the real lesson is the people who come our way and don't laugh off our trauma. The ones who hold your hand in the darkness, don't call you a hungry thing when you are struggling. Don't dismiss you as tragedy and instead hug you close through the moments of too much. Don't think you're too much when you need love. The ones who would punch through a wall if it meant finding you on the other side, and will defend you behind your back, who will not let any hunter take aim at you when you are not looking. Won't let you see yourself as a hunted thing and have the courage to call you out when you are the one doing the hunting. Maybe the real gift is the friends we made along the way. The ones who can see us at our ugliest, stained sweatshirt, make-up-free, tear-streaked face after a break-up and say, 'You're beautiful, clown. You always will be and I love you. Now have a shower – you stink.'

I. WHEN YOU SEE YOUR FRIEND BEING CRUEL TO SOMEONE

You watch as their once flower mouth
turns poisonous, rotting roses
falling from their lips that turn into wasps,
stinging the quiet, gentle person before you both,
someone who doesn't deserve it,
someone who has done no one any harm
and that's what has made them an easy target.
You want to tell your friend to stop.
You want the warrior in you to do something.
But you do nothing.
Just stand there and watch.

II. THESE ARE THE WORDS YOU SHOULD HAVE SAID

Look,
I know everything has felt like
a punch in the gut lately,
that you should have aced that test,
your mum shouldn't have yelled at you that way,
your dad's words should have been kinder,
but there is no healing
in making someone else suffer.
You're taking all the pain given to you
and shoving it on to someone else
and you may think it'll help you feel better,
but it won't, not like this,
because all it is doing is making you cruel.
All it is doing is turning you
into what we have always said we have hated.
You are still the person
who once walked two miles
to take a wounded bird to shelter,
bandaged its wing and taught it to fly again.
That is who you are.
Remember that.

III. AND THIS IS WHY YOU DIDN'T

When we watch horror movies, we deride the people within
them. Pretend we know better. Think we are smarter. We
wouldn't make those mistakes, wouldn't go looking into the
mouth of evil, would defend our loved ones differently, but
real life doesn't work like that. In real life when we see someone
we thought we knew well do something completely out of
the ordinary, it's like watching them become a monster before
our eyes and we freeze. It's why you froze too. Witnessing
someone gentle turn violent would do that to you. Suddenly you
understand all the people in the horror films you once named
small. You realize that in a place of fear, a place of the unknown,
we all act similar in many ways. The next time this happens,
you will know exactly how to be brave. But the first time? Allow
yourself some grace for not knowing what to say.

WHEN GHOSTING HURTS MOST

She's the sister you never had. You know her favourite colour and what breaks her heart. She knows why you like odd socks and the name of the first person who shattered your confidence. You spend every waking moment together, know every secret, every joke, every unhealed wound. And then, slowly, she stops responding to your messages. She stops taking your calls. You see her and she barely notices you. You'll see her talking to a new girl with the joy she once only had for you and your bones will ache. We are creatures desperate for closure. But no amount of asking or begging makes her tell you what you did wrong.

Here is the answer: nothing. You did nothing wrong. She outgrew you, but didn't have the language to tell you. In her inability to communicate, she ended up being cruel. I know this answer is unsettling, I know this isn't closure, but the best thing you can do in this situation is walk away, and understand that you deserve better than a friend who treats you that way.

TELL ME AGAIN

About your wins,
about the time when you got it all right,
about all the things that hurt you
that made you fall in love,
about everyone who stayed and left.

It is a joy to hear you speak
and know everything about you.
If friendship is anything,
it is this, it is this,
it is this.

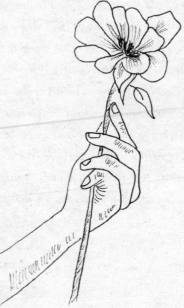

THEY LIED WHEN THEY SAID ONLY ROMANTIC BREAK-UPS HURT

When your friend breaks up with you, you'll feel like you want to die. Like your heart has shattered. And yet, despite the pain, you're still here. This isn't just surviving. It's surviving losing one of the greatest loves of your life, a love no one wants to acknowledge. You feel like kindling after a fire. You feel like a tree destroyed by lightning. You feel like a city deserted by all those who once lived in it. Is there any cure for the emptiness? The whole of history is full of people searching for cures that are never to be found. You'll read about Alfred Lord Tennyson so devastated by the loss of his friend that he sank into depression for ten years. Of Van Gogh cutting his ear off as an offering to the God of rage after a friend abandoned him. You realize there is no cure to grief but love. So you put away your friendship. You learn to love it in crystallized moments. Once upon a time, you remember, someone loved me so much we did everything together. And then you learn how to grieve for someone who is still alive somewhere across the world and wish them well.

SOULMATE

Everything you read will tell you
that a soulmate is someone you love

in a very particular way, but as you get older
you realize how fortunate you are

because one person can have
a thousand soulmates.

A soulmate for when you want to look
at the night sky.

A soulmate for dancing
all through the long, glittering night.

A soulmate you can tell every secret to
and know they will keep them.

A soulmate to go on long drives
where the cool breeze makes you feel alive.

A soulmate who you know so well
you finish each other's sentences.

A soulmate who sits by your mother's bedside
with you when she gets sick.

A soulmate who you put your arm round
at their father's funeral.

A soulmate who shares
their grandmother with you.

A soulmate who stands by you
when you feel your life is over.

A soulmate who sees you at your worst
and helps you clean up the mess after.

The difference is, you don't call them a soulmate.
You name them friend.

THE GLOW

You're supposed to meet to do homework,
but homework doesn't happen,
because you're having so much fun.

So you forget the books and deep-dive
into everything else:
girlhood and politics and love

and parents and dreams that you
would never ever tell anyone.
And somewhere while you're talking

you see it, that glow that rises
from their skin and yours
as you understand for the first time

this is what found families are made of.

US

It's not a feeling,
it's just knowing
that no matter what we do
there will be us.

The queens of spring,
fixing each other's crowns,
protecting each other
from anyone who brings us down.

We are here to cheer each other on
and there is no purer love than this,
the love of sisters who found each other,
rejoicing in what belongs to us,

Life, a brand-new adventure;
friendship, a cathedral we built together
where our love becomes prayer
where every laugh is an amen.

AUTHOR'S NOTE

This book covers heavy things because to be a human is heavy with love, loss, joy, chaos, truth and beauty. I wanted you to feel seen in all the huge and terrible things just as much as I wanted you to feel seen in your joy. To feel, after all, is the greatest gift we are given, even if it doesn't always feel that way. But keeping in mind how much grief and trauma is discussed in this book, there are good places that can help you recover in moments of tragedy and intense pain.

SAMARITANS
Confidential support for people experiencing feelings of distress or despair.
Telephone: 116 123 (free 24-hour helpline)
Website: www.samaritans.org/

ANXIETY UK
Charity providing support if you have been diagnosed with an anxiety condition.
Telephone: 03444 775 774
(Monday to Friday, 9.30am to 5.30pm)
Website: www.anxietyuk.org.uk

NO PANIC

Voluntary charity offering support for sufferers of panic attacks and obsessive compulsive disorder (OCD). Offers a course to help overcome your phobia or OCD.

Telephone: 0300 772 9844 (daily, 10am to 10pm). Calls cost the same as a 01 or 02 numbers and are included in minutes packages.

Website: www.nopanic.org.uk

YOUNGMINDS

Information on child and adolescent mental health. Services for parents and professionals.

Telephone: Parents' helpline 0808 802 5544
(Monday to Friday, 9.30am to 4pm)

Website: www.youngminds.org.uk/

RAPE CRISIS

To find your local services phone: 0808 802 9999 (daily, 12pm to 2.30pm and 7pm to 9.30pm)

Website: www.rapecrisis.org.uk

CRUSE BEREAVEMENT CARE

Telephone: 0808 808 1677 (Monday to Friday, 9am to 5pm)

Website: www.cruse.org.uk/home

All contact details are correct at the time of publication.

ACKNOWLEDGEMENTS

It takes a village to make an author and it takes an even bigger village to make a book, especially one like this, which is full of so many experiences that have affected me so deeply. Without good people in my life to lean on, I would not be the woman, or indeed the writer I am today.

It is with this in mind that I thank:

My parents and my brother for their love always.

Sim for her tireless hard work and for helping craft this book into a piece of work I am so proud of.

Gaby for believing in me and this book.

My agent Niki Chang for forever being my champion.

Nikesh, Anoushka, Salena, Chimene, Nerm, Gnarly, Sangna, Trista, Anita, Sophia, Dean, Reju, Manjeet, Aakash, Nabihah, Nadine, Mahogany, Roger, Joelle, Carlos, Sunny, Emma, Lauz, Heather, Iain, Matt, Faye, Dave, Rebekah, Clara, Annie, Clare, Layla, Alison, Shaun – you are forever my favourite human beings, and I am blessed to know you.

And Steve, who has never, ever stopped believing in me. Every time I speak of good loves, I am talking about you.

ABOUT THE AUTHOR

Nikita Gill is a British-Indian poet, playwright, writer and illustrator living in the south of England. She has published five collections of poetry: *Your Soul is a River* (Thought Catalog), *Your Heart is the Sea* (Thought Catalog), *Wild Embers* (Trapeze), *Fierce Fairytales* (Trapeze) and *Great Goddesses* (Ebury).

She is the editor of the poetry anthology *SLAM!* (Macmillan Children's Books) and a novel in verse called *The Girl and Goddess* was published by Ebury on National Poetry Day 2020.